Where that bear?

Liz Lewis

Geographical Association

Nan and Grandpa give Barnaby a new camera.

He takes it with him on a field trip to Edinburgh.

In Edinburgh they visit Arthur's Seat.
'Where is Barnaby?' asks Mrs Glass.

'Click' goes Barnaby's camera.
'Oh. There he is!'

I was just waiting for the sun to come out.

Photo: Margaret Mackintosh

Next day they visit the castle.
'Where has Barnaby gone?' asks Mrs Glass.

'Click' goes Barnaby's camera.
'Oh. There he is!'

I was just waiting for those people to move.

They have a picnic in Princes Street Gardens.
'Is Barnaby missing again?' puffs Mrs Glass.

I w
waitir
cloud

'Click' goes Barnaby's camera.
'Oh. There he is!'

ust
r that
nove.

On the way home they go to see two big bridges.

Mrs Glass is cross. She tells Barnaby he must not go away.

11

'Click, click, click, click, click' goes the camera. 'The bridges are too long. I can't see them all from here!' Barnaby grumbles.